THE MEDITERRANEAN DIET FOR KIDS

How To Get Kids On the Mediterranean diet

Emelda G Smith

THE MEDITERRANEAN DIET
FOR *KIDS*

Emelda G. Smith

COPYRIGHT PAGE

All rights reserved. No part of this publication may be reproduced, distributed, or transmitted in any form or by any means, including photocopying, recording, or other electronic or mechanical methods, without the prior written permission of the publisher, except in the case of brief quotations embodied in critical reviews and certain other noncommercial uses permitted by copyright law.

Copyright © Emelda G. Smith , 2023.

TABLE OF CONTENT

Copyright Page..............................

Table Of Content...............................

Introduction ....

Chapter 1: Healthy Eating Habits..............

Chapter 2: Health Benefits Of Mediterranean Diet..............................

chapter 3: How To Start A Mediterranean Diet Plan.......................................

Chapter 4: How To Get Kids On A Mediterranean Diet.................................

Chapter 5: Mediterranean Diet Recipes For kids ....

Conclusion

FOREWORD

One of the most effective methods to expose your children to the Mediterranean diet is through cooking. The simplicity of the Mediterranean diet is one of its best features. Calorie and fat grams counting is not necessary. Also, you don't need to stop eating any of your favorite meals. Just be certain that the majority of the items you consume are on the list of permitted foods.

The Mediterranean diet is defined in this book by Emelda G. Smith, along with its health benefits and how youngsters can

INTRODUCTION

The Mediterranean diet has been around for centuries and is still popular today. It is well known for its delicious flavors and vibrant colors that make it stand out from other diets. It is a way of eating that is based on the traditional foods of the Mediterranean region, which includes countries like Italy, Greece, and Spain. This diet is rich in fruits, vegetables, whole grains, legumes, nuts, and healthy fats. It also includes moderate amounts of fish, poultry, and dairy products.

preparing a healthier future for your children right away!

It may help introduce youngsters to the world of healthy eating in a fun way thanks to its straightforward, delectable recipes, wholesome ingredients, and kid-friendly approaches. In order to help them choose their food wisely, it is also packed with nutrition recommendations and cooking instructions. This book is certain to become a family favorite in the kitchen!

nutrients that are crucial for your child's health and development. Fruits and vegetables are a good source of fiber, vitamins, and minerals; whole grains are a good source of complex carbohydrates and essential vitamins and minerals; olive oil is a good source of fat; and fish is a good source of protein and omega-3 fatty acids, which are crucial for brain development, heart health, type 2 diabetes prevention, obesity prevention, and the prevention of some cancers and other chronic diseases. Also, it can enhance children's academic performance and foster cognitive health.

Breakfast, lunch, dinner, and snacks are all covered in the recipes, making it simple to incorporate a Mediterranean diet into your family's daily routine. And even people who are finicky eaters will like the dinners because they are so delicious!

So why are you still waiting? With these excellent recipes from the Mediterranean Diet Cookbook for Kids, you can start benefit from adopting it. The book also offers advice on how to begin a Mediterranean diet, including how to choose healthy foods and prepare quick, scrumptious meals. Children are meant to be introduced to the nutritious and delectable foods of the Mediterranean diet through the recipes in this book. All of the foods are simple to make and nutrient-dense, making them ideal for children's developing bodies. The Mediterranean diet is not only healthy, but also delicious! These nutritious ingredients can be used in a wide variety of cuisines. Family cooking sessions are a wonderful way to strengthen relationships and impart good eating practices to kids.

Start your children off on the Mediterranean Diet if you want them to eat healthfully. It's a fantastic approach to get kids started on a lifestyle and lifelong healthy eating habits.

The Mediterranean diet is abundant in fish, whole grains, fruits, vegetables, and olive oil. These nutritious foods include vital

This diet emphasizes the importance of eating a variety of foods, in moderation, and limiting processed foods.

The Mediterranean diet is also known for its health benefits, including reducing the risk of heart disease, type 2 diabetes, and some types of cancer. It is also associated with a lower risk of obesity, high blood pressure, and other chronic conditions. This diet can also help you maintain a healthy weight, as well as improve your mental and emotional wellbeing. These foods are high in fiber and other essential nutrients, which can help reduce the risk of chronic diseases.

The Mediterranean diet is filled with fresh fruits and vegetables, whole grains, lean proteins, and healthy fats. It is one of the healthiest diets out there for children. It's a diet loaded with fresh fruits, vegetables, whole grains, nuts, and healthy fats like olive oil. It's rich in vitamins and minerals, and may help youngsters adopt good eating habits from an early age.

This book is full of delicious recipes that will introduce kids to the Mediterranean diet. Each recipe is designed to be easy to make, healthy, and tasty. The recipes are also designed to be kid-friendly, with kid-friendly ingredients, so that kids can enjoy their meals. With these recipes, kids can learn how to cook healthy, delicious meals and get excited about eating the Mediterranean way.

The Mediterranean diet also offers several health advantages. It's been linked to decreasing the risk of obesity, diabetes, and heart disease, and it may help youngsters maintain a healthy weight. In this booklet,

We will discuss the basics of the Mediterranean diet, including what foods are included, the health benefits, and meal planning tips. We'll examine the advantages of the Mediterranean diet, and share tasty

and healthy recipes for children

CHAPTER 1: HEALTHY EATING HABITS

The first step to introduce a Mediterranean diet to children is to create good eating habits. Educating children to make good food choices, and to eat in moderation, is crucial. Encourage them to eat a variety of foods, including fruits, vegetables, whole grains, nuts, and healthy fats. Limiting foods that are high in sugar, salt, and saturated fats is also important. It's also important to get children involved in meal planning and preparation. Let them help pick out recipes, and involve them in the cooking process. This can be a great way to teach them about nutrition, and to help them understand the importance of eating a healthy diet.

Here are some healthy eating habits for kids on the Mediterranean diet:

Encourage plenty of fruits and vegetables: Fruits and vegetables are a key part of the Mediterranean diet. Encourage your kids to eat a variety of colorful fruits and vegetables every day, try including different types of fruits and vegetables in meals and snacks.

Choose whole grains: Whole grains are another important part of the Mediterranean diet. Choose whole-grain bread, pasta, rice, and other grains instead of refined grains.

Include Healthy Fats:

The Mediterranean diet includes healthy fats like olive oil, nuts, and seeds. Encourage your kids to eat foods that contain healthy fats and limit foods that are high in saturated and trans fats.

Eat Fish And Seafood: The Mediterranean diet includes fish and seafood as a source of protein. Try to include fish and seafood in meals at least twice a week.

Limit processed foods: The Mediterranean diet emphasizes fresh, whole foods and limits processed foods. Encourage your kids to choose whole, minimally processed foods instead of highly processed snacks and meals.

Encourage family meals: The Mediterranean diet emphasizes the importance of family meals. Try to eat meals together as a family as often as possible.

Drink water: Water is the best choice for staying hydrated. Encourage your kids to drink water throughout the day and limit sugary drinks like soda and juice.

Remember, healthy eating habits are important for everyone, but they are especially important for kids who are still growing and developing. By following the Mediterranean diet and encouraging healthy eating habits, you can help your kids develop lifelong healthy habits

CHAPTER 2: HEALTH BENEFITS OF MEDITERRANEAN DIET.

The Mediterranean diet is a way of eating that is based on the traditional dietary patterns of countries bordering the Mediterranean Sea. This type of diet emphasizes whole foods, such as fruits, vegetables, whole grains, legumes, nuts, and seeds, and healthy fats like olive oil, while limiting processed foods, red meat, and sugary drinks.Numerous studies have shown that the Mediterranean diet can help improve various aspects of health.

The Mediterranean diet is not only beneficial for adults but also for children. Here are some of the health benefits of the Mediterranean diet for children:

Improved cardiovascular health: The Mediterranean diet emphasizes whole grains, fruits, vegetables, fish, and healthy fats, which can improve cardiovascular health and reduce the risk of heart disease in children.

Reduced risk of obesity: The Mediterranean diet is rich in fruits, vegetables, and whole grains, which are low in calories but high in fiber, helping to prevent obesity in children. The high content in fiber and low processed foods and sugar helps to promote weight loss and maintenance in children also.

Reduced risk of heart disease: The Mediterranean diet is rich in heart-healthy foods, such as fruits, vegetables, whole grains, fish, and olive oil, which have been shown to reduce the risk of heart disease.

Lowered risk of diabetes: The Mediterranean diet can help improve blood sugar control and insulin sensitivity, which can reduce the risk of developing type 2 diabetes.

Improved cognitive function: The Mediterranean diet is associated with improved cognitive function in children, including better memory and attention span.

Reduced risk of asthma and allergies: The Mediterranean diet's emphasis on fruits, vegetables, nuts, and fish may help reduce the risk of asthma and allergies in children.

Improved bone health: The Mediterranean diet includes calcium-rich foods such as dairy products, leafy greens, and fish, which can improve bone health in children.

Reduced risk of certain types of cancer: The diet is rich in antioxidants and anti-inflammatory compounds, which can help reduce the risk of certain types of cancer.

Lower risk of depression: Studies have found that the Mediterranean diet is associated with a lower risk of depression in children.

Helps establish healthy eating habits: A Mediterranean diet emphasizes whole, nutrient-dense foods, which can help children establish healthy eating habits early in life. By introducing children to a variety of healthy foods, parents can encourage their children to enjoy a diverse range of flavors and textures, making it more likely that they will continue to choose healthy foods as they grow older. Overall, a Mediterranean diet can offer a range of health benefits for children, from promoting healthy growth and development to reducing the risk of chronic diseases. Parents can help their children establish healthy eating habits by emphasizing whole, nutrient-dense foods, and by modeling healthy eating behaviors themselves.

Foods to Eat and Avoid on the Mediterranean Diet

The Mediterranean diet emphasizes a wide variety of whole, nutrient-dense foods, while limiting processed and refined foods. Here are some foods to eat and avoid on the Mediterranean diet:

Foods to Eat: Fruits and vegetables: Aim for at least five servings of fruits and vegetables per day.

Whole grains: Choose whole grains such as brown rice, quinoa, whole wheat bread, and whole grain pasta.

Legumes: Include lentils, chickpeas, beans, and peas in your meals.

Nuts and seeds: Enjoy a handful of nuts or seeds as a snack or add them to meals for a boost of healthy fats and protein.

Fish and seafood: Aim for at least two servings of fish per week, choosing fatty fish such as salmon, mackerel, and sardines.

Poultry: Enjoy chicken and turkey in moderation.

Dairy products: Include yogurt and cheese in moderation.

Foods for children to Avoid on the Mediterranean Diet

1. Avoid sugary processed cereals and breakfast bars.
2. Avoid processed meats such as hot dogs, bologna and lunch meats.
3. Avoid foods high in saturated fats such as fried foods, chips, and fast food.
4. Avoid white breads, pastas and other refined grains.
5. Avoid sugary drinks such as soda, energy drinks, and fruit juices.
6. Avoid sweets such as candy, cookies, and cakes.
7. Avoid processed snacks such as chips and crackers.

8. Avoid high-sodium canned and processed foods.
9. Avoid artificial sweeteners and additives.
10. Avoid processed cheese, cream cheese, and other cheese products

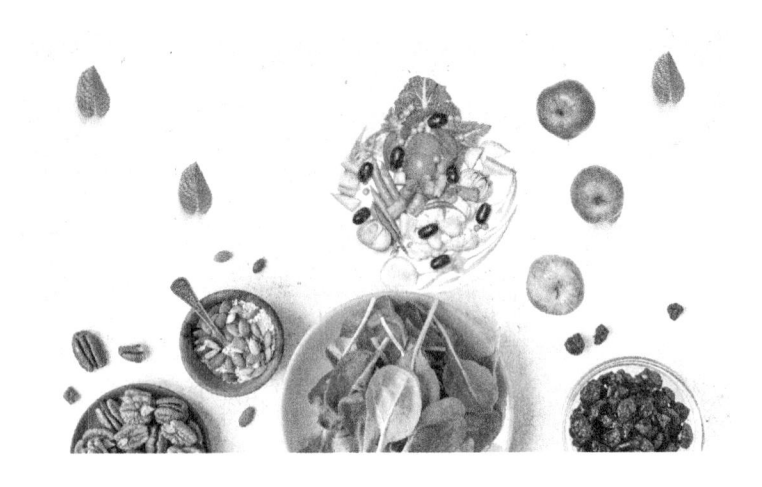

CHAPTER 3: HOW TO START A MEDITERRANEAN DIET PlAN

Concentrate on whole foods: The Mediterranean diet does not typically include processed items. Choose foods like bulgur or oats that include just one to three whole-food ingredients. Whole foods include fruits, vegetables, entire grains, nuts, legumes, fish, and olive oil.

Make veggies the primary course of every meal: The majority of your meals should consist of fruits and vegetables. Even 3 to 5 servings of fruits and vegetables per day have been found to lower the risk of cardiovascular disease, which is what the Mediterranean diet promotes at 6 to 10 daily servings. Consider minor changes you may make to your meals to include more vegetables, such as slathering avocado and cucumber on your sandwich and opting for an apple and nut butter as a snack rather than crackers

Replace red meat with fish instead: The main sources of protein in the Mediterranean diet are fatty fish like salmon, mackerel, tuna, and herring. High quantities of omega-3 fatty acids found in these fish help lower inflammation and raise cholesterol levels. You can have moderate servings of chicken, turkey, eggs, cheese, and yogurt once a week or every day.

Replace butter with olive oil: Olive oil is the primary source of fat in the Mediterranean diet, therefore use it while cooking instead of butter. The type of fat is more significant than total fat. The Mediterranean diet places a strong emphasis on increasing the consumption of poly- and monounsaturated fats while reducing the consumption of saturated and trans fats. Trans fat and saturated fat both increase LDL cholesterol. To lower your cholesterol and improve the health of your heart, substitute butter for heart-healthy fats like olive oil.

Rethink your dairy: In America, people frequently put cheese on everything. Aim to consume a range of tasty cheeses in moderation rather than slathering it on everything. Avoid processed cheeses like American and choose instead strong-flavored varieties like feta or parmesan (a tiny amount is sufficient).

Enjoy yogurt, but wherever feasible, stick with plain, fermented, and Greek varieties.

Avoid flavored, high-sugar yogurts since too much-added sugar is bad for your health.

Switch white rice and pasta with nutritious grains: Switching your white rice and pasta with nutritious grains like bulgur, barley, and farro to replace processed grains helps in the regulation of blood sugar. A staple of the Mediterranean diet, whole grains have many health advantages, including decreasing cholesterol, and aiding in weight loss. Also rich in fiber and B vitamins are whole grains.

Legumes and beans are both included in the Mediterranean diet and have similar health advantages.

Eat some nuts as a snack: Nut fat is nothing to be alarmed about. Nuts are rich in poly- and monounsaturated fats, the good fats, like olive oil and avocados. They also contain fiber and protein. The ideal combination for feeling full, regulating blood sugar, lowering cholesterol, and reducing inflammation are fat, protein, and fiber. Between lunch and dinner, eat a quarter cup of nuts. Most omega-3s are found in walnuts, however, other nuts contain good fats. If you need more to be satisfied, combine them with a fruit or vegetable.

Learn to Avoid sugar most of the time: The Mediterranean diet does not include and discourages frequent consumption of processed foods like cookies, crackers, refined flour, and sweets. Save the ice cream and cookies for special occasions. People in the Mediterranean region moderately indulge in sweets like gelato and baklava. In the absence of that, they consume fresh fruit, such as dates and figs, to quell their sugar cravings.

Veggies & Fruits: For the best nutrition, select a range of hues and shop during the appropriate season.

Fruits include the following, as examples: Berries, Apples, Bananas, Oranges, Pears, Clementines, Cherries, Grapes, Avocado

,Apricots, Figs, Tomatoes ,Beets, Onions ,Zucchini, Peppers, Peas and lots more

Fish

A crucial component of the Mediterranean diet is fish. As opposed to other meat protein sources, try to consume more fish. You can consider the following examples; Sardines, herring, mackerel, tuna, salmon, and tuna or any other seafood you

Dairy is acceptable in moderation on the Mediterranean diet.

Ricotta, Parmesan, feta, and other natural cheeses, greek yogurt as well as plain yogurt Legumes, Seeds, and Nuts

Various options are available for snacks, salad toppings, and more.

Spices & Herbs

Get a range of these to add flavor to your meals rather than relying solely on the saltshaker. Although dry herbs are as tasty as fresh, simply use less of them.

CHAPTER 4: HOW TO GET KIDS ON A MEDITERRANEAN DIET

You won't be able to change your child's eating habits overnight, but you can take the following actions to increase the Mediterranean influence of your child's meals and snacks:

Improve the drip. Does your child dribble creamy salad dressing over his baby carrots? Replace this condiment with hummus, which is lower in calories, added sugar, sodium, and saturated fat.

Home-made pizza. Make pizza by using a thin whole-grain crust. Add whatever vegetable your child enjoys on top, even corn.

Begin consuming more seafood.

Eat fish and seafood frequently if you're following the Mediterranean diet. Give your child the opportunity to try seafood when there is no pressure, such as at a buffet or when she is taking a bite of your food. Eventually, work your way up to homemade fish. When you're ready to move on to the fish, grill some and top it with a fruit salsa your kids love.

Vegetables and picky eaters

Typically, whole and mashed potatoes are the only vegetables that 30% of one-year-olds consume

Vegetables are the most finicky of all the foods that youngsters may be. This is caused in part by the natural bitterness of vegetables, which many kids must gradually learn to like.

The other issue is that kids might not be exposed to a wide range of vegetables served in various ways often enough.

Vegetables Must Look Appetizing

Another study sheds light on the reasons behind kids' resistance to veggies.

For youngsters to be willing to try new food (which might be licking, tasting, chewing, or eating), it has to look nice and taste well, according to flavor and taste preference studies.

Boost the success of vegetables.

Once your child starts enjoying a wide variety of fruits and vegetables. You should boost the likelihood that he'll eat more of it.

Pair a favorite with something unknown or less preferred (such as corn with red onions, cucumbers with radishes, or watermelon with baby spinach). As salads can be difficult to sell, start with mild butter lettuce and incorporate lots of tasty, well-known toppings (like dried fruit, sunflower seeds, or orange wedges). If salads are sliced, kids would like them more. Even though it takes more time to prepare, the result will be a happy, healthier eater.

Avoid butter and red meat.

Red meat, such as beef, lamb, and pork, is extremely rarely included in the Mediterranean diet. Use high-fiber beans or seafood to receive the necessary amount of protein. Olive oil is a heart-healthy alternative to butter. Also learn to satisfy your child's snacking needs with nuts, low-fat cheese, yogurt, fresh fruit, and vegetables.

10 Unique Vegetable Serving Ideas for Children

I have numerous ideas for serving vegetables to youngsters that will help pique their curiosity about trying them and foster a lifelong habit of eating them.

1. Use a dip for vegetables.

Using a dip can be a way to tempt even the pickiest eaters, from traditional Ranch dressing to homemade Greek yogurt-based varieties. Try salsa, guacamole, nut butter, peanut sauce, ketchup, black bean dip, salsa, and even hummus!

2. Roasted Veggies

Vegetables' inherent sweetness is brought out when they are roasted. The secret lies in caramelization, a chemical reaction that "browns" vegetable sugars and releases a sweet, nutty flavor. Bitter is gone; gentle sweetness is here! Give these roasted carrots a try!

3. Don't Cook Them Too Long

I once observed one of my relatives prepare green beans. She began preparing them at 3:30 PM and didn't serve them until 6:00 PM! They spent more than two hours cooking on the stove. She had added bacon and onions, and they were good, but they were mushy.

Vegetables should be blanched or cooked till tender-crisp for children. Despite being heated and thoroughly cooked, they will still have a "pop" when your youngster bites into them.

4. Include Flavors

Even fat and salt may make dull, flavorless vegetables into something delectable to eat.

Examples are butter, olive oil, vegetable oil, and a sprinkle of salt.

5. Use fruits to sweeten Salad

Fruit can be used to sweeten salads for dinner. To increase color and encourage consumption, add strawberries, blueberries, peach, or orange slices to your salads.

To maintain the flavor's fresh, light, and zesty quality, toss with some olive oil and a spritz of lemon juice.

6. Skewer vegetables.

Boring vegetables look appetizing when served with cheese cubes and vegetables on a stick. Instead of using long skewers, use tiny toothpicks, and keep an eye on your children!

7. Young Vegetables

Have you noticed the sprouting of baby vegetables?

Baby artichokes, baby eggplant, baby peppers, baby carrots, and so forth.

Compared to their mature relatives, these "baby" varieties have a milder flavor and, in the case of lettuces, a softer, more sensitive texture.

8. Choose sweeter vegetables.

If you need to introduce vegetables to your child gradually, pick the tastiest varieties you can find.

The best vegetables to choose first are yams, sweet potatoes, squash, peas, and carrots.

9. Use Vegetables to Create a Pretty Image

A smart vegetable-based artwork will be difficult for toddlers and preschoolers to resist. Use your imagination when drawing faces, schools, houses, flowers, or trees.

Watch as some of the vegetables he uses to create his picture end up in his mouth!

10. Don't hide them; just blend them in.

Smoothies are a favorite food of many kids. And while I am not a huge believer in "hiding" veggies, blending some spinach or kale into a fruit smoothie is a great way to enhance nutrition and include vegetables in delightful ways.

Do not forget to include your child in the smoothie-making process! See the vegetables vanish as you blend after having him/her add them.

CHAPTER 5: MEDITERRANEAN DIET RECIPES FOR

Here we will be discussing how to prepare mediterranean diets ranging from appetizers, desserts to soups and main dishes; the ingredients needed and instructions to follow.

Appetizers
Mediterranean Hummus

This easy-to-make hummus is full of flavor and is perfect for dipping vegetables or pita chips and it's a simple and delicious way to enjoy fresh and healthy ingredients. Here's how you can make it at home for your lovely kids:

Ingredients:
1 can chickpeas, drained and rinsed
2 cloves garlic, minced
2 tablespoons tahini
2 tablespoons lemon juice
1/4 teaspoon cumin
2 tablespoons olive oil

Instructions on how to prepare Mediterranean hummus

1. In a food processor, combine the chickpeas, garlic, tahini, lemon juice, and cumin. Process until the mixture is smooth.
2. With the processor running, slowly add the olive oil and process until combined.
3. Serve with pita chips or vegetables.

Mediterranean Baked Feta

Preparing a baked feta is a simple and delicious way to enjoy healthy ingredients. This flavorful appetizer is sure to be a hit with your lovely kids; here's how you can make it at home for your them:

Ingredients:
1 block feta cheese
1/4 cup olive oil
2 tablespoons oregano
2 cloves garlic, minced
1/2 teaspoon red pepper flakes

Instructions on how to prepare Mediterranean baked feta
1. Preheat the oven to 350°F.
2. Place the feta in an oven-safe dish and pour the olive oil over it. Sprinkle the oregano, garlic, and red pepper flakes over the top.
3. Bake for 15-20 minutes, until the feta is golden brown and bubbly.
4. Serve with pita chips or vegetables.

Greek Salad Skewers

Thread cherry tomatoes, cucumbers, feta cheese, olives, and red onions onto skewers. Serve with a side of Greek yogurt dip.

Ingredients:

-1/2 cucumber
-1/2 red onion
-1/2 red pepper
-1/2 yellow pepper
-1/2 cup feta cheese
-1/4 cup olives
-1/4 cup olive oil
-2 tablespoons red wine vinegar
-1 teaspoon oregano
-salt and pepper to taste

Instructions on how to prepare Greek Salad Skewers

1. Start by washing and preparing all of the vegetables. Chop the lettuce, dice the cucumber and bell pepper, thinly slice the red onion, and dice the tomatoes.

2. In a bowl, combine the cucumber, red onion, red pepper, yellow pepper, feta cheese, and olives.

3. In a separate bowl, whisk together the olive oil, red wine vinegar, oregano, and salt and pepper.
4. Pour the dressing over the vegetable mixture and toss to combine.
5. Preheat the grill to medium-high heat.
6. Thread the vegetables onto skewers, alternating between each vegetable.
7. Grill the skewers for 8-10 minutes, flipping occasionally, until the vegetables are lightly charred.
8. Serve the Greek salad skewers warm or at room temperature. Enjoy!.

You can also choose to add other Mediterranean ingredients to your salad such as artichoke hearts, roasted red

Mediterranean Pita Pizza

Preparing a Mediterranean Pita Pizza is a simple and delicious way to enjoy fresh and healthy ingredients and is a perfect choice for your children. Here's how you can make it at home for your lovely kids:

Ingredients:

-1 package of pre-made pita bread
-1/2 cup of your favorite marinara sauce
-1/4 cup of feta cheese
-1/4 cup of black olives, chopped
-1/4 cup of red onion, thinly sliced
-1/4 cup of artichoke hearts, chopped
-1/4 cup of sun-dried tomatoes, chopped
-1/2 cup of mozzarella cheese, shredded
-1/4 cup of fresh basil, chopped

Instructions on how to prepare Mediterranean Pita Pizza

1. Preheat the oven to 375 degrees.
2. Place pita bread on an ungreased baking sheet.
3. Spread marinara sauce evenly over each piece of pita bread.
4. Top with feta cheese, black olives, red onion, artichoke hearts, and sun-dried tomatoes.
5. Sprinkle mozzarella cheese over the top.
6. Bake in a preheated oven for 10-15 minutes, or until the cheese is melted and bubbly.

7. Remove from the oven and top with fresh basil.
8. Slice and serve. Enjoy!

Roasted Red Pepper Hummus

This delicious hummus recipe is made with roasted red peppers, chickpeas, garlic, and tahini, and it's perfect for dipping or spreading on sandwiches and wraps.

Ingredients:
2 red bell peppers
1 15-ounce can chickpeas, drained and rinsed
1/4 cup tahini
2 cloves garlic, minced
2 tablespoons fresh lemon juice
2 tablespoons extra-virgin olive oil
1/2 teaspoon ground cumin
1/2 teaspoon smoked paprika
1/4 teaspoon sea salt
1/4 teaspoon black pepper
Optional garnish:
1 tablespoon chopped fresh parsley

Instructions on how to prepare Roasted Red Pepper Hummus

1. Preheat your oven to 400 degrees Fahrenheit.
2. Cut the red bell peppers in half and remove the seeds. Place them cut-side down on a baking sheet. Roast for 30-35 minutes or until the peppers are charred and soft.
3. Place the roasted peppers in a food processor and blend until smooth.
4. Add the chickpeas, tahini, garlic, lemon juice, olive oil, cumin, smoked paprika, salt, and pepper to the food processor and blend until smooth.
5. Taste and adjust the seasonings to your liking.
6. Transfer the hummus to a serving bowl.
7. Garnish with chopped fresh parsley, if desired. Serve with pita chips, sliced vegetables, or crackers. Enjoy!

Zucchini Fritters

Preparing Mediterranean zucchini fritters is a simple and delicious way to enjoy fresh and healthy ingredients. Here's how you can fo about making it at home for your lovely kids:

Ingredients:
-2 cups grated zucchini
-1/4 cup all-purpose flour
-1/4 cup grated Parmesan cheese
-1 egg, beaten
-1/4 teaspoon garlic powder
-1/4 teaspoon onion powder
-Salt and pepper, to taste
-Vegetable oil, for frying

Instructions on how to prepare Zucchini Fritters

1. Place the grated zucchini in a strainer and press down with a spoon to remove any excess moisture.
2. In a medium bowl, mix together the zucchini, flour, Parmesan, egg, garlic powder, onion powder, salt, and pepper.
3. Heat the oil in a large skillet over medium-high heat.

4. Using a tablespoon, scoop up a heaping spoonful of the zucchini mixture and drop it into the hot oil.
5. Fry the fritters for 3-4 minutes, flipping occasionally, until they are golden brown.
6. Remove the fritters from the oil and place them on a paper towel-lined plate to drain.
7. Serve the fritters hot with your favorite dipping sauce. Enjoy!

Mediterranean Grilled Cheese

Preparing a Mediterranean cheese is a simple and nutritious way of enjoying God and healthy food, good for you lovely kids; here's how you can make it at home:

Ingredients:
2 slices of whole grain bread
2 slices of mozzarella cheese
2 slices of tomato
4 slices of cucumber
1 tablespoon of olive oil
1 tablespoon of hummus
1 teaspoon of oregano

Instructions on how to prepare Mediterranean Grilled cheese

1. Preheat a non-stick skillet over medium-high heat.
2. Brush one side of each slice of bread with the olive oil.
3. Place the bread oil side down onto the skillet.
4. Place the cheese slices onto the bread.
5. Place the tomato and cucumber slices onto one slice of the bread.
6. Spread the hummus onto the other slice of bread.
7. Sprinkle the oregano on top of the vegetables.
8. Carefully flip one slice of bread onto the other, making sure to keep the vegetables and cheese in the center.
9. Grill the sandwich for 3-4 minutes on each side, until the cheese is melted and the bread is golden brown.
10. Serve the Mediterranean grilled cheese hot. Enjoy!

Mediterranean Wraps

This flavorful appetizer is sure to be a hit with kids. ow to prepare Mediterranean Wraps

Ingredients:
- 4 Whole-Wheat Tortillas
- 2 cups Shredded Romaine Lettuce
- 1/2 cup Chopped Cucumber
- 1/2 cup Chopped Red Onion
- 1/2 cup Chopped Tomatoes
- 1/2 cup Chopped Kalamata Olives
- 1/2 cup Crumbled Feta Cheese
- 1/4 cup Chopped Fresh Parsley
- 1/4 cup Olive Oil
- 2 tablespoons Fresh Lemon Juice
- Salt and Pepper, to taste

Instructions on how to prepare Mediterranean Wraps

1. Heat the tortillas in a dry skillet over medium-high heat for 1-2 minutes per side, or until lightly toasted and pliable.

2. In a medium bowl, combine the lettuce, cucumber, red onion, tomatoes, olives, feta cheese, and parsley.
3. In a small bowl, whisk together the olive oil, lemon juice, salt, and pepper.
4. To assemble the wraps, spread a spoonful of the dressing over each tortilla. Top with a generous scoop of the salad mixture.
5. Fold the bottom of the tortilla up and over the salad, then fold the sides in towards the center and roll the wrap up tightly.
6. Serve immediately or wrap in plastic wrap and refrigerate until ready to serve. Enjoy!

Mediterranean Quesadillas

Mediterranean quesadillas are a tasty twist on a classic Mexican dish, you can also enjoy your Mediterranean quesadillas as an appetizer, snack, or light meal. Here's how you can make this nutritious and delicious dish at home to enjoy with your lovely kids:

Ingredients
- 4 (7-inch) flour tortillas
- 1/2 cup crumbled feta cheese

- 1/2 cup chopped kalamata olives
- 1/4 cup diced red onion
- 1/2 cup diced roasted red peppers
- 1/4 cup olive oil
- 1 teaspoon garlic powder
- Salt and pepper to taste

Instructions on how to prepare mediterranean quesadillas

1. Preheat a large skillet over medium heat.
2. Place 2 tortillas on a cutting board.
3. Sprinkle half of the feta cheese, olives, red onion, and red peppers evenly over each tortilla.
4. Drizzle each tortilla with 1 tablespoon of olive oil.
5. Sprinkle garlic powder, salt, and pepper over each tortilla.
6. Place the remaining 2 tortillas over the topping on each of the tortillas.
7. Carefully place the quesadillas in the preheated skillet and cook for 3-4 minutes per side until the tortillas are golden brown and the cheese is melted.

8. Cut each quesadilla into wedges and serve. Enjoy!

Prosciutto-Wrapped Asparagus

Prosciutto-wrapped asparagus is a simple and delicious appetizer that's perfect for any occasion. Here's how you can make it at home for your lovely kids:

Ingredients:
- 12-16 asparagus spears, trimmed
- 4 slices prosciutto
- 2 tablespoons olive oil
- Salt and pepper, to taste

Instructions on how to prepare Prosciutto-Wrapped Asparagus

1. Preheat the oven to 375 degrees F.
2. Line a baking sheet with parchment paper.
3. Place the asparagus spears on the baking sheet. Drizzle with olive oil and season with salt and pepper.
4. Wrap each asparagus spear with a slice of prosciutto.

5. Bake in a preheated oven for 12-15 minutes, or until prosciutto is crispy and asparagus is tender.
6. Serve hot. Enjoy!

Mediterranean Cheese Platter

A Mediterranean cheese platter is a perfect addition to any meal. Here's how you can create a delicious and appealing cheese platter using Mediterranean ingredients which is good for your wonderful and lovely kids:

ingredients:

-Cheese (such as feta, manchego, blue cheese, etc.)

-Olives (such as kalamata, Castelvetrano, etc.)

-Dried fruits (such as apricots, figs, dates, etc.)

-Nuts (such as almonds, walnuts, pistachios, etc.)

-Crackers or sliced bread

-Hummus

-Extra virgin olive oil

2. Arrange the cheeses on the platter. Make sure to have a variety of different types and flavors.
3. Place the olives around the cheeses.
4. Add the dried fruits and nuts.
5. Place the crackers/bread slices around the platter.
6. Add a small bowl of hummus.
7. Drizzle extra virgin olive oil over the platter.
8. Serve and enjoy!

Desserts

Mediterranean Fruit Salad

This simple and tasty dessert is sure to be a hit with kids.

Ingredients:

2 cups mixed fruit (such as apples, oranges, grapes, strawberries, etc.)
1/4 cup honey
2 tablespoons lemon juice
2 tablespoons olive oil
2 tablespoons fresh mint, chopped

Instruction on how to prepare mediterranean fruit salad:

1. In a large bowl, combine the fruit.
2. In a small bowl, whisk together the honey, lemon juice, olive oil, and mint.
3. Drizzle the dressing over the fruit and toss to combine.
4. Serve chilled.

Greek Salad with Feta and Olives

This delicious and healthy salad is packed with flavor and crunchy veggies, topped with feta and olives and It is a great way of getting your kids to eat their vegetables!

Ingredients:

2 large ripe tomatoes, chopped
1/2 cucumber, diced
1/4 red onion, sliced
1/2 cup feta cheese, crumbled
1/4 cup pitted kalamata olives, halved
2 tablespoons olive oil
2 tablespoons red wine vinegar
1 teaspoon dried oregano

Salt and pepper to taste

Instructions on how to prepare Mediterranean greek Salad with Feta and Olives

1. In a large bowl, combine the tomatoes, cucumber and red onion.
2. Add the feta cheese and olives, and mix gently.
3. In a small bowl, whisk together the olive oil, red wine vinegar, oregano, salt and pepper.
4. Pour the dressing over the salad and toss gently to combine.
5. Serve immediately or chill in the refrigerator for up to 2 hours before serving. Enjoy!

Mediterranean Chickpea Salad

This easy to prepare and delicious salad is a great way to introduce your kids to the delicious and nutritious flavors of the Mediterranean. It's also packed with protein and fiber, so it's a healthy choice for your kids!

Ingredients:

1 can chickpeas, drained and rinsed
1 cup grape tomatoes, halved
1/4 cup diced red onion
1/4 cup chopped fresh parsley
2 tablespoons freshly squeezed lemon juice
2 tablespoons extra-virgin olive oil
1 teaspoon dried oregano
1/4 teaspoon garlic powder
Salt and freshly ground black pepper, to taste
1/4 cup crumbled feta cheese

Instructions on how to prepare Mediterranean Chickpea Salad

1. In a large bowl, combine chickpeas, tomatoes, red onion, and parsley.
2. In a small bowl, whisk together the lemon juice, olive oil, oregano, and garlic powder. Season with salt and pepper to taste.
3. Pour the dressing over the chickpeas and toss to combine.

4. Sprinkle feta cheese over the top and serve. Enjoy!

Mediterranean Potato Salad

Kids will love this creamy potato salad with its Mediterranean flavors. It's a great side dish for any meal, and it's packed with healthy potatoes tossed with crunchy vegetables and other nutritious ingredients. Kids will love it!

How to prepare Mediterranean Potato Salad

Ingredients:

2 lbs. red potatoes, cut into 1/2 inch cubes
1/4 cup red onion, chopped
1/2 cup black olives, pitted and chopped
1/4 cup fresh parsley, chopped
1/4 cup extra-virgin olive oil
2 tablespoons lemon juice
2 cloves garlic, minced
1 teaspoon Dijon mustard
Salt and pepper to taste

Instructions on how to prepare Mediterranean Potato Salad

1. Place the potatoes in a large pot and cover with cold water. Bring to a boil over medium-high heat and cook for 8-10 minutes until fork-tender. Drain and rinse under cold water, then set aside.
2. In a large bowl, combine the potatoes, onion, olives, and parsley.
3. In a small bowl whisk together the olive oil, lemon juice, garlic, mustard, salt, and pepper.
4. Pour the dressing over the potato mixture and toss to coat.
5. Serve immediately or store in the refrigerator for up to 3 days. Enjoy!

Panzanella Mediterranean Salad

Panzanella Mediterranean salad is a mix of crunchy vegetables, like cucumbers and peppers, fresh tomatoes, olives, as well as feta cheese. It's then topped with a tangy dressing made of olive oil, vinegar, and herbs. It is also a great way to use up stale bread - just tear it up and add it to the salad for a delicious crunch.

Ingredients:

2 large tomatoes, diced
2 cups cubed day-old bread
1/2 cup kalamata olives, pitted
1/2 cup shredded fresh basil leaves
1/4 cup extra-virgin olive oil
2 tablespoons red wine vinegar
1 tablespoon freshly squeezed lemon juice
1/4 teaspoon sea salt
1/4 teaspoon freshly ground black pepper
1/4 cup crumbled feta cheese

Instructions on how to prepare panzanella mediterranean salad

1. Preheat your oven to 400°F.
2. Place the cubed bread on a baking sheet and bake for 12-15 minutes or until golden brown and toasted.
3. Place the diced tomatoes, olives, basil, olive oil, red wine vinegar, lemon juice, salt, and pepper in a large bowl. Mix until all the ingredients are combined.

4. Add the toasted bread cubes, and toss together with the other ingredients.
5. Serve the panzanella salad immediately or add feta cheese and serve. Enjoy!

Mediterranean Baba Ganoush

Baba ganoush is an easy to make, delicious Mediterranean appetizer made from eggplants, tahini, and other spices. It is creamy, flavorful and perfect for dipping your favorite crunchy veggies or chips into. It is also full of vitamins and antioxidants which is good for your kid!

Ingredients:
2 medium eggplants
2 cloves of garlic, minced
2 tablespoons of tahini
2 tablespoons of lemon juice
1/4 teaspoon of cumin
Salt and pepper, to taste
3 tablespoons of extra-virgin olive oil
Fresh parsley or mint, finely chopped (optional)
Pita bread or vegetable sticks, for serving

Instructions on how to prepare baba ganoush Mediterranean appetizers

1. Preheat your oven to 400°F.
2. Cut the eggplants in half lengthwise and score the flesh with a knife in a crisscross pattern.
3. Brush the cut sides of the eggplants with olive oil and season with salt and pepper. Place the eggplants cut-side down on a baking sheet and bake for about 20 minutes, or until the eggplants are softened and slightly charred.
4. Remove from the oven and allow the eggplants to cool.
5. Once cooled, scoop the flesh of the eggplants into a bowl.
6. Add the garlic, tahini, lemon juice, cumin, salt

Tabbouleh Mediterranean Salad

Mediterranean salad is a delicious and nutritious salad that is packed with fresh and tasty ingredients. Such as salad bulgur wheat, fresh vegetables like tomatoes and cucumbers, lots of parsley, and some olive oil, lemon juice, and salt to bring out the flavor. It's also a great way to get your greens. And you can choose to add in some other veggies you like, like carrots or peppers.

Ingredients:

2 cups cooked bulgur wheat
1/2 cup chopped parsley
1/2 cup chopped mint
1/4 cup diced red onion
1/4 cup diced cucumber
1/4 cup diced red bell pepper
1/4 cup diced tomato
1/4 cup crumbled feta cheese
2 tablespoons freshly squeezed lemon juice
2 tablespoons extra-virgin olive oil
1 teaspoon minced garlic
Salt and freshly ground black pepper, to taste

Instructions on how to prepare tabbouleh mediterranean salad

1. In a medium bowl, combine the cooked bulgur wheat, parsley, mint, red onion, cucumber, bell pepper, tomato, and feta cheese.
2. In a small bowl, whisk together the lemon juice, olive oil, garlic, salt, and pepper.
3. Pour the dressing over the bulgur wheat mixture, and toss to combine.
4. Serve the tabbouleh salad at room temperature, or chill in the refrigerator for 1-2 hours before serving. Enjoy!

Mediterranean Tuna Salad

This is a light and refreshing tuna salad that is packed with flavor and healthy proteins. It's perfect for a quick lunch or dinner, and definitely kids will love the combination of tuna, olives, and capers.

Ingredients:

2 cans of tuna in water, drained
1/4 cup diced red onion
1/4 cup pitted kalamata olives, sliced
1/4 cup diced red bell pepper
2 tablespoons fresh parsley, chopped
2 tablespoons extra virgin olive oil

2 tablespoons red wine vinegar
1 tablespoon fresh lemon juice
1 teaspoon dried oregano
Salt and pepper to taste

Instructions on how to prepare Mediterranean tuna salad

1. In a medium-sized bowl, combine the tuna, red onion, olives, red bell pepper, and parsley.
2. In a small bowl, whisk together the olive oil, red wine vinegar, lemon juice, and oregano. Pour the dressing over the tuna salad and stir to combine.
3. Taste and season with salt and pepper as desired.
4. Serve the salad on a bed of greens, or with your favorite crackers or bread. Enjoy!

Mediterranean Yogurt Parfait

This dessert is tasty, healthy and nutritious, it is perfect for busy days. Kids will love the combination of yogurt, granola, and fresh fruit.

Ingredients:
2 cups plain yogurt
1/2 cup fresh fruit (such as strawberries, blueberries, etc.)
1/2 cup granola
2 tablespoons honey

Instructions on how to prepare mediterranean yogurt parfait:
1. In a bowl, layer the yogurt, fruit, and granola.
2. Drizzle the honey over the top.
3. Serve chilled.

Soups and Salads
Mediterranean Bean Soup

This soup is loaded with fiber and protein. Kids will really love the combination of white beans, tomatoes, and a variety of herbs and spices.

Ingredients:
2 tablespoons olive oil

1 onion, diced
2 cloves garlic, minced
1 can diced tomatoes
2 cans white beans, drained and rinsed
4 cups vegetable broth
1 teaspoon oregano
1 teaspoon basil

Instructions on how mediterranean bean soup:

1. Heat the olive oil in a large pot over medium heat. Add the onion and garlic and sauté until softened, about 5 minutes.
2. Add the diced tomatoes, beans, and vegetable broth and bring to a boil. Reduce the heat and simmer for 15 minutes.
3. Stir in the oregano and basil and simmer for another 5 minutes.
4. Serve hot.

Mediterranean Salad

Mediterranean salad is a healthy and nutritious way to introduce your kids to the flavors of the Mediterranean. It's filled with fresh ingredients like cucumbers, tomatoes, olives, feta cheese, and herbs that will make your kids smile. It is not only full of flavor, but it also has plenty of health benefits for your child's growing body.

Ingredients:

2 cups mixed greens

1/2 cup cherry tomatoes, halved

1/2 cup cucumber, chopped

1/4 cup olives, pitted and halved

1/4 cup feta cheese

2 tablespoons olive oil

1 tablespoon lemon juice

1 teaspoon oregano

Instructions on how to prepare Mediterranean salad

1. In a large bowl, combine the greens, tomatoes, cucumber, olives, and feta cheese.
2. In a small bowl, whisk together the olive oil, lemon juice, and oregano.
3. Drizzle the dressing over the salad and toss to combine.
4. Serve chilled.

Main Dishes
Mediterranean Baked Fish

This healthy and delicious dish is sure to be a hit with kids and is perfect for a weeknight meal. It's easy to make and full of flavor. Kids will love the combination of herbs, lemon, and garlic.

Ingredients:

2 tablespoons olive oil

4 (4-ounce) white fish filets

1/2 teaspoon salt

1/2 teaspoon pepper

1 lemon, sliced

2 cloves garlic, minced

2 tablespoons fresh parsley, chopped

Instructions on how to prepare mediterranean baked fish

1. Preheat the oven to 350°F.

2. Heat the olive oil in a large oven-safe skillet over medium heat. Add the fish filets and season with salt and pepper.

3. Place the lemon slices and garlic around the fish and sprinkle the parsley over the top.
4. Bake for 15-20 minutes, until the fish is cooked through.
5. Serve hot.

Mediterranean Stuffed Peppers

This is only a delicious recipe but also a healthy recipe that is perfect for your kids. It involves stuffing bell peppers with a mix of ground beef, onion, garlic, tomatoes, and herbs. The peppers are then topped with cheese and baked in the oven for a delicious and nutritious meal

Ingredients:

4 large bell peppers
1 tablespoon olive oil
1 onion, diced
2 cloves garlic, minced
1 can diced tomatoes
1 can black beans, drained and rinsed
1 cup cooked rice
1/2 teaspoon oregano

1/2 teaspoon basil

1/2 cup grated cheese

Instructions on how to prepare Mediterranean stuffed peppers

1. Preheat the oven to 375°F.
2. Cut the peppers in half lengthwise, remove the seeds. Place the peppers in a baking dish and set aside.
3. Heat the olive oil in a large skillet over medium heat. Add the onion and garlic and sauté until softened, about 5 minutes.
4. Add the diced tomatoes, beans, and cooked rice and stir to combine. Simmer for 5 minutes.
5. Remove the skillet from the heat and stir in the oregano, basil, and cheese.
6. Stuff the pepper halves with the mixture and bake for 20-25 minutes, until the peppers are tender.
7. Serve hot.

Mediterranean Roasted Vegetables:

This is a great way to get your kids to eat

their vegetables. Roasting a variety of vegetables in the oven with olive oil, garlic, and herbs creates a flavorful and nutritious dish that kids will love.

Ingredients:
2 bell peppers, sliced
2 zucchini, sliced
2 yellow squash, sliced
1 large onion, sliced
1/4 cup olive oil
1 tablespoon Italian seasoning
1/2 teaspoon garlic powder
1/2 teaspoon salt
1/4 teaspoon black pepper L

Instructions on how to prepare mediterranean Roasted Vegetables
1. Preheat the oven to 400°F.
2. In a large bowl, combine bell peppers, zucchini, yellow squash, and onion.
3. Drizzle olive oil over vegetables and season with Italian seasoning, garlic powder, salt, and pepper.

4. Line a large baking sheet with parchment paper and spread vegetables in a single layer.

5. Roast vegetables in a preheated oven for 25-30 minutes, stirring halfway through, until vegetables are lightly browned and tender.

6. Serve warm and enjoy!

Mediterranean Greek Style Potatoes

This recipe is flavorful, fun and perfect for kids. It involves baking potatoes in the oven with garlic, oregano, and feta cheese, creating a delicious and nutritious side dish.

Ingredients:

3-4 large potatoes, peeled and cut into wedges

1/4 cup olive oil

3 cloves garlic, minced

1 teaspoon dried oregano

1/2 teaspoon dried thyme

1/2 teaspoon smoked Spanish paprika

Salt and pepper to taste

1/4 cup crumbled feta cheese
1/4 cup chopped fresh parsley

Instructions on how to prepare Greek style potatoes:
1. Preheat the oven to 400 degrees F.
2. Place the potato wedges in a large bowl and drizzle with olive oil.
3. Add the garlic, oregano, thyme, and smoked Spanish paprika and season with salt and pepper. Toss to coat.
4. Transfer the potatoes to a baking sheet lined with parchment paper and spread out in a single layer.
5. Bake in the preheated oven for 30-35 minutes, or until golden and crispy.
6. Sprinkle with feta cheese and parsley and serve. Enjoy!

CONCLUSION

Establishing a Mediterranean diet for your children doesn't have to be tough. Here are some pointers to help you get started:

1. Select whole grain versions of meals, such as whole wheat pasta, quinoa, and brown rice.
2. Incorporate lots of fresh fruits and vegetables.
3. Utilize healthy fats like olive oil and nuts.
4. Minimize processed and sugary meals.
5. Get your children involved in meal planning and preparation.

The Mediterranean diet is a healthful and tasty diet for children. It's full with fresh fruits and vegetables, whole grains, nuts, and healthy fats. It offers several health advantages, and may help youngsters adopt good eating habits from an early age.

With these recipes, kids can learn how to cook healthy, delicious meals and get excited about eating the Mediterranean way. From appetizers and soups to main dishes and desserts, each recipe is designed to be easy to make, healthy, and tasty. Eating the Mediterranean way can help reduce the risk of chronic diseases and promote overall health, so get cooking and enjoy the delicious flavors of the Mediterranean diet!

With the recipes and tips provided in this ebook, you'll be able to create a Mediterranean diet for your children. You'll be able to provide them with delicious and nutritious meals that will help them lead a healthy and active lifestyle

The Mediterranean Diet Cookbook For kids

Printed in Great Britain
by Amazon